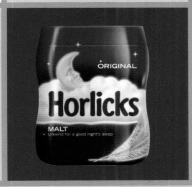

# The Horlicks Cookbook

## Paul Hartley

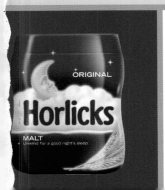

# The Horlicks Cookbook

**Paul Hartley**

In association with
**www.breakfastandbrunch.com**

First published in Great Britain
in 2010
by **Absolute Press**
Scarborough House
29 James Street West
Bath BA1 2BT England
**Phone** 44 (0) 1225 316013
**Fax** 44 (0) 1225 445836
**E-mail** info@absolutepress.co.uk
**Website** www.absolutepress.co.uk

**Publisher**
Jon Croft
**Commissioning Editor**
Meg Avent
**Art Direction & Design**
Matt Inwood and
Claire Siggery
**Photography**
Matt Inwood
**Food Stylist**
Andrea O'Connor

A catalogue record of this book
is available from the British Library

**ISBN** 9781906650315

Printed and bound in Slovenia on
behalf of Latitude Press.

The Horlicks trade marks and
copyrighted materials used in this
book are owned exclusively by the
GlaxoSmithKline group of
companies or are used with
permission.

# CONTENTS

**1869**

William Horlick from Ruardean, Gloucestershire emigrated to the United States.

**1873**

James Horlick, a pharmacist, joined his brother, William, in the U.S. and together they founded the company J&W Horlicks in Chicago to manufacture a patented malted milk drink as an artificial infant food.

**1875**

Business moved to larger premises at Racine, Wisconsin, with an abundant supply of spring water.

**1883**

U.S. patent 278,967 granted to William for first malted milk drink mixing powder with hot water.

**1908**

Construction completed on the UK factory built in Slough, England at a cost of £28,000.

# Horlicks

**1935**

James made a baronet. First World War – use of Horlicks drink at home and at the front.

**1914**

Death of James. Company splits. William now responsibile for the Americas and James' sons for rest of world.

**1921**

Richard E. Byrd named the Horlick Mountains on the edge of the Ross Ice Shelf after William, in appreciation of his support. A small factory opens in Australia for the local market, including New Zealand.

**1945**

The U.S. company was acquired by the British Horlicks business.

**1960**

Factory built in India to make Horlicks from buffalo milk.

**1968**

Factory built in Punjab, Pakistan.

# Milestones

**1928**

William Horlick High School in Racine, Wisconsin opens its doors on September 18th!

William Horlick dies on September 25th 1936, in Racine, Wisconsin, USA, aged 90.

**1936**

# The **Horlicks** Collection

# Horlicks Brownies

We all love brownies but these, made with lots of malty milk flavour, are especially delicious.

**MAKES 9 BROWNIES**

200g plain chocolate (minimum 70% cocoa solids)
250g salted butter, chopped into 8 chunks
$1/2$ teaspoon vanilla extract
350g caster sugar
$1/4$ teaspoon baking powder
25g cocoa powder
65g plain flour
4 tablespoons **Horlicks Original powder**
4 medium free-range eggs

**You will need some baking parchment and a suitable oven tray, approximately 24x30cm and 4cm deep**

Preheat the oven to 180°C/350°F/ Gas Mark 4.

Bring a pan of water to a simmer and place either a Pyrex or metal bowl on top of the pan. Break in the chocolate and add the butter, stirring occasionally until it's all melted. Once the chocolate and butter are melted stir in the vanilla. Remove the bowl from the heat.

In a separate bowl, sift together the sugar, baking powder, cocoa powder, flour and the Horlicks. Mix them together well and then fold into the melted chocolate mixture until a heavy paste is formed. Now add the eggs and mix until smooth and glossy – this is important!

Line the base and sides of the tray with baking parchment and spread the mixture evenly. Place the tray in the oven and cook for 15–20 minutes until the slightest crust has formed on the surface.

Leave to cool completely, this will take 4–5 hours. With a sharp knife, cut into 9 equal portions and serve. To make it even more special, place a fresh strawberry on each piece and dust with icing sugar

# Horlicks Tiffin

Tiffin originated in British India as an afternoon snack and is a delicious treat; perfect with a cup of Darjeeling tea. Malt and chocolate in perfect harmony.

100g unsalted butter
4 tablespoons golden syrup
50g cherries, destoned and
   chopped
50g raisins
2 heaped tablespoons drinking
   chocolate powder
2 heaped tablespoons **Horlicks**
   **Original powder**
200g pack of malted milk biscuits
50g Maltesers
200g dark chocolate

**You will need a square tin, approximately 18x18cm lined with foil**

In a saucepan, melt the butter and golden syrup, then add the cherries, raisins, drinking chocolate powder and Horlicks. Stir all these together over a medium heat – it is important not to let the mixture boil.

Pop the malted biscuits into a bag and crush gently with a rolling pin until broken into small pieces – you want pieces, not crumbs.

Take the saucepan off the heat, then add the biscuits and Maltesers and stir well. Tip into the lined tin and spread into the corners lightly, pressing down with a spatula, then leave to cool completely.

Finally, melt the dark chocolate in a heatproof bowl over a pan of boiling water and pour over the top, tilting the tin from side to side, end to end, to spread evenly, then allow to set completely.

Remove from the tin, peel off the foil and cut on a board into bite-sized bars. Serve on a pretty dish with a sprig of fresh mint.

## IN THE BEGINNING

Born in Gloucestershire in 1846, William Horlick gave up his job as a saddlemaker to seek a new life in America. He worked in a Chicago quarry run by his cousin. In 1873, younger brother, James, a pharmacist, who apprenticed for a baby food company in England, joined him in America. He arrived with an idea that would become the malted milk drink we love!

# Brunch Pancake Stack

### A SIGHT FOR SLOUGH EYES...

The UK Horlicks factory based in Stoke Poges Lane in Slough (opposite) is one of the more beautiful historical industrial buildings still standing today. It has been operational since 1908.

These are thick American-style pancakes with Horlicks in the batter. Sandwiched with pineapple and topped with juicy redcurrants, this dish makes the perfect brunch!

**MAKES 12–14 PANCAKES**

**For the pancakes**
285g plain flour
2 teaspoons baking powder
$\frac{1}{2}$ teaspoon salt
2 tablespoons caster sugar
2 tablespoons **Horlicks Original powder**
275ml full-fat milk
3 medium free-range eggs
50g unsalted butter, melted and cooled

**For the filling**
25g butter
12 pineapple slices
1 tablespoon Demerara sugar
golden syrup or maple syrup, to serve
4 sprigs redcurrants, to serve

Into a bowl sift the flour, baking powder, salt, caster sugar and Horlicks and mix together. Put the milk, eggs and butter into a separate bowl and whisk by hand. Add the dry ingredients to the milk mixture and whisk together gently. Don't worry if the mixture isn't too smooth. You can leave the batter for a while or even overnight, ready for the morning.

Heat a large, lightly-greased frying pan (or use a griddle if you have one) and add two tablespoons of the batter to achieve a pancake roughly 10cm in size. Cook over a medium heat for about a minute or until bubbles appear on the surface of the pancake. Flip the pancake over and cook for a further minute until golden. Cook all the batter in batches of 3–4 or as your pan allows, adding a little more oil as needed. Wipe the pan around with a pad of kitchen paper to remove excess oil. Keep the pancakes warm in the oven as you make them.

In a separate frying pan, melt the butter and sauté the pineapple rings until golden, sprinkling them with the Demerara sugar whilst cooking to caramelise them. Again, you may need to do this in batches.

Now onto each plate place one pancake, then one pineapple ring and repeat until you have a stack of three of each. Drizzle with syrup, arrange a small bunch of redcurrants on top of each and serve immediately.

# Horlicks Chocolate Cream Roulade

This is a truly delicious roulade with Horlicks at every turn giving it a deep, rich malted flavour. This makes a scrumptious afternoon treat.

## For the sponge
3 medium free-range eggs
125g golden caster sugar
75g self-raising flour, sifted
25g ground almonds
2 heaped tablespoons **Horlicks Original powder**

## For the chocolate cream
100g butter
50g cream cheese
25g cocoa powder
150g icing sugar
2 heaped teaspoons **Horlicks Original powder**

extra golden caster sugar and **Horlicks Original powder** for dusting

**You will need a Swiss roll tin, approximately 23x30cm and some baking parchment**

Pre-heat the oven to 180°C/350°F/ Gas Mark 4.

You can do this by hand in a mixing bowl but it's much easier if you use a food processor. In a mixer or bowl beat together the eggs and the golden caster sugar until pale and thick and the beater leaves a trail when lifted. Next, gently fold in the flour, ground almonds and the Horlicks.

Pour into the Swiss roll tin, spreading gently into the corners and cook in the centre of the oven for approximately 15 minutes. Meanwhile, mix all the ingredients for the chocolate cream together in a mixing bowl and beat well. Set aside.

After 15 minutes, remove the tin from the oven and tip out onto a piece of greaseproof paper sprinkled with caster sugar and Horlicks. Allow to cool. Spread the chocolate cream all over, then, taking the edge of the greaseproof paper, gently form the cake into a roll removing the greaseproof paper as you go. The cream will keep it in shape. Dust with cocoa powder to finish.

**Horlicks HINTS**

**A slice of this roulade makes a perfect dessert served alongside a nice cold scoop of peppermint ice cream.**

# Buttercream Sponge Cake

Horlicks makes this into the most scrumptious fluffy sponge cake ever!

**For the sponge**
200g self-raising flour
1 teaspoon baking powder
100g ground almonds
1 heaped tablespoon **Horlicks Original powder**
75g light brown sugar
50g golden caster sugar
2 medium free-range eggs, beaten
250ml natural yoghurt
2 tablespoons sunflower oil
4 teaspoons **Horlicks Original powder**, dissolved in 2 tablespoons of hot water and left to cool

**For the buttercream filling**
2 tablespoons golden caster sugar
2 heaped tablespoons **Horlicks Original powder**
125g light mascarpone cheese
100g quark cheese
1 tablespoon icing sugar
$\frac{1}{2}$ teaspoon vanilla essence

**For the icing**
125g royal icing sugar
1 teaspoon **Horlicks Original powder**

**You will need a 23cm loose-bottom cake tin lined with baking parchment**

Preheat the oven to 180°C/350°F/ Gas Mark 4.

Sift the flour into a mixing bowl, stir in the baking powder, ground almonds, Horlicks Original powder and both sugars and rub out any sugar lumps with your fingers. Make a well in the centre and put in the eggs, yoghurt, oil and dissolved Horlicks. Stir with a wooden spoon until evenly mixed.

Pour the mixture into the tin, smooth it over to level the mix and bake for 40–45 minutes, or until the top springs back when touched. Remove from the oven and allow to cool for a short time then turn out onto a wire rack and allow to cool completely.

When completely cool, peel off the baking parchment and split the cake into two layers.

Make a syrup for the filling by putting caster sugar and Horlicks into a small heavy-based pan and add three tablespoons of water. Heat gently while stirring until the sugar is dissolved. Raise the heat until the syrup boils and keep boiling for 2–3 minutes, until it has thickened, then pour into a small bowl to cool. Once cool it should be like treacle.

Beat the mascarpone, quark, icing sugar and vanilla essence together until smooth then stir in the Horlicks syrup mixing well to incorporate and set aside.

Sift the royal icing sugar into a bowl, mix the Horlicks with a tablespoon of warm water to dissolve then mix into the icing sugar and beat well. Add a drop more water if required. Spread the filling onto the bottom layer of the sponge and place on the top layer. Finally, spread the royal icing onto the top of the cake.

# Keep Horlick's on your shelves

and you will never be at a loss for a readily prepared food-drink for one and all, be they children or old folk. Horlick's Malted Milk has its place on the table, in the nursery and in the sick-room. Every woman should be familiar with its valuable properties. Horlick's is a complete food for infants—it promotes growth in children and aids the recovery of the sick. It is an excellent pick-me-up. Horlick's is a well-balanced combination of milk, wheat and malted barley, very nourishing and easily digested. Made in a moment with either hot or cold water.

## HORLICK'S
### THE ORIGINAL
## MALTED MILK

In 4 sizes
of all Bazaars & Stores

HORLICK'S MALTED MILK Co., Ltd., Slough, Bucks., Eng.

# Letter to Lord's:

Dear .....

Here's to Lord's. Hope you're all feeling fit. Hope you've been sleeping
well. Hope you've all been having Horlicks.

Did the players who made their mark at Old Trafford drink Horlicks?
We don't know. But we do know that if you sleep better you feel fitter.
And that Horlicks helps.

Fall asleep each night easily, peacefully. Sleep soothed and nourished.
Wake up each morning knowing your sleep has done you good.

Sleep better, feel better, play better. Best wishes,

Yours every night,

**Comforting, creamy Horlicks,
the food-drink of the night**

**Well taken!**

---

# Letter to all Wimbledon players:

Dear .....

The best of luck for the tournament. No strained wrists or
nerves, we hope! Have you been sleeping well? Have you been
having Horlicks?

Stupid of us to claim that Horlicks can make all the difference
to that match point. But not stupid of us to remind you that if
you sleep better you feel fitter. And that Horlicks helps.

Fall asleep easily, peacefully. Sleep soothed and nourished.
Wake up each morning knowing your sleep has done you good.
Sleep better, feel better—serve, run, volley better. Best wishes.

Yours every night,

**Comforting, creamy Horlicks,
the food-drink of the night**

**Serve Horlicks!**

---

# Letter to all Derby jockeys:

Dear ...

Good luck at Epsom. Hope you're all feeling fit. Hope you've all been sleeping well.
Hope you've all been having Horlicks.

Stupid of us to claim that Horlicks will get you the Gold Cup. But not stupid of us
to remind you that if you sleep better you feel fitter. And that Horlicks helps.

Fall asleep easily, peacefully. Sleep soothed and nourished. Wake up each morning
knowing your sleep has done you good.

Sleep better, feel better, ride better. Good luck !

Yours every night,

**Comforting, creamy Horlicks,
the food-drink of the night**

**P.S. Is your horse sleeping well?**

Daily Mirror   23 May 1966

# Breakfast Banana Smoothie

Smoothies make a great breakfast, and did you know that bananas and yoghurt together make a great hangover cure?

You'll need a basic electric blender or a smoothie maker to make this delicious and nourishing breakfast in less than two minutes.

**MAKES 1 PINT**

1 banana, broken into 4 chunks
2 level tablespoons **Horlicks Original powder**
2 tablespoons runny honey (if you warm the spoon first it really helps)
400g natural yoghurt
4 ice cubes

Peel the banana the night before, wrap it in cling film and pop it into the freezer. This helps to chill the smoothie and adds extra texture.

Put all the ingredients into the blender and whiz for 30 seconds. Serve in tall glasses.

## HIP HORLICKS

In recent years, Horlicks has been spotted on the bar menus of some of the country's more trendy venues. At London's famed Groucho Club, it appears as the winding down tipple of choice, rubbing shoulders with Cristal Champagne and a bevvy of different cocktails.

# TiramaHorlicks

**THE DIET OF CHAMPIONS!**

Or so declared this leaflet from the 1928 Amsterdam Olympic Games. Horlicks could be found around the city in various cafés and restaurants in all of the competitive areas and was being provided free of charge to the competitors of all nations for the duration of the Games.

Summer nights and Italian food are a marriage made in heaven – this TiramaHorlicks will have Italian chefs desperate to call it their own. It's truly delicious.

**SERVES 6–8**

15 sponge fingers (depending on the size of your dish)
1 double espresso coffee
30ml Amaretto liqueur
6 free-range egg yolks
100g icing sugar
3 tablespoons **Horlicks Original powder**
750g mascarpone cheese
cocoa powder, for dusting
dark chocolate, for shavings

**You'll need a dish approximately 25x15cm, 5cm deep**

Lay the sponge fingers out to cover the bottom of the dish. Mix the coffee and Amaretto together and pour it all over the biscuits.

In a bowl, whisk together the egg yolks, icing sugar and Horlicks until thick and creamy. Add the mascarpone a little at a time whisking it well into the mix to make sure there are no lumps.

Pour the mixture over the soaked sponge fingers and refrigerate for at least 2 hours until it is set.

Finally, dust with a thick layer of cocoa powder, shower with dark chocolate shavings and serve.

AMSTERDAM 1928

## At the Invitation of the Dutch Olympic Committee

# HORLICKS

### The Diet of Champions.

For many years Horlicks has been used by an ever increasing number of the World's greatest Athletes and Sportsmen as the most important item of their diet whilst training for the particular sports at which they have excelled.

There are on file hundreds of spontaneous letters from World's, British and American Champions and Record Holders in various branches of Sport who attribute the successes gained very largely to the physical fitness and the wonderful stamina built up by the regular use of this food-drink.

### The Secret of Success.

The story is a simple one. One of the greatest secrets of success in Sport and Athletics lies in the rapid replacement of the tissue broken down, and the energy expended during strenuous effort. Unless this replacement is quickly accomplished there is a danger of staleness and over-strain. Horlicks makes good this wastage far more efficiently than any other item of diet, because every particle of it is whole-some, easily digested nourishment of which the nutritive ratio is balanced to perfection.

### The Meal before Practice.

The best results are achieved when the Athlete makes Horlicks the chief item of the light meal taken previous to exercise. It is completely assimilated in a very short space of time and moreover aids in the digestion of the solid food eaten. Horlicks is, therefore, an invaluable help in preventing the vomiting which so often occurs after a great effort due to undigested food remaining in the stomach.

**will be served FREE to the competitors of all nations from stalls adjacent to the dressing-rooms at the Stadium.**

In Horlicks full-cream English milk is combined with the soluble nutritive extracts of the choicest malted barley and wheat-flour. During the process of manufacture the constituents are thoroughly pasteurised, the casein of the milk is rendered easily digestible, and the starch of the grains is converted into highly nutritious dextrine and maltose.

It contains in correct proportions all the nutritive elements demanded by nature to support life and maintain health, energy and vitality. It is so quickly and easily digested that it may be taken even during strenuous exertion, and its ample nourishment is so rapidly appropriated by the whole system that its benefits are felt immediately.

### In the Dressing-room.

Another glass of Horlicks, preferably hot, should be sipped in the dressing-room immediately after exercise. Its balanced nourishment restores metabolism by feeding the system back to normality and thereby assures the digestive energy necessary for the proper assimilation of a subsequent meal.

### And Last Thing at Night.

Then a glass of Horlicks, hot, should be sipped before retiring. It will feed and soothe the nerve centres, and by so enabling the nerves to rest, will assure sound, refreshing sleep, and the light yet ample nourishment thus taken will help to build up that welcome reserve of energy which so often makes all the difference to the Athlete towards the end of a hard fought contest.

### Fitness Wins.

It is to the regular use of Horlicks, as above described, that so many World's and Olympic Champions and Record Holders attribute the winning of their laurels. Horlicks is indeed the Diet of Champions—the food of physical fitness.

## Served in the principal cafés and restaurants everywhere

# Banoffee Cheesequake

Totally indulgent but extra-specially tasty with a delicious Horlicks toffee sauce. Serve just chilled for a really special dessert treat.

**For the base**
12 digestive biscuits, crushed
25g melted butter

**For the toffee sauce**
125g butter
6 tablespoons Demerara sugar
2 teaspoons golden syrup
2 tablespoons **Horlicks Original powder**
75ml double cream

**For the topping**
500g mascarpone cheese
100ml double cream
juice of $\frac{1}{2}$ lemon
2 heaped teaspoons icing sugar
2 egg whites
50g milk chocolate, chopped into small pieces
2 bananas, sliced

**You will need a 25cm-diameter, 8cm-deep loose-base tin that has been lightly greased**

Combine the crushed biscuits and melted butter until they stick together and then press this into the base of the tin. Put this in the freezer to set.

To make the toffee sauce, melt the butter in a pan and add the sugar and syrup. Once mixed together and smooth, add the Horlicks and cream, stir well again and then leave to cool and refrigerate.

Put the mascarpone, cream and lemon juice into a bowl and mix together. Sieve in the icing sugar and slowly fold it into the mixture until it is smooth and creamy. In a separate, very clean bowl whisk the egg whites into stiff peaks. Fold this into the mascarpone mixture.

Remove the biscuit base from the freezer and arrange the banana slices over the base. Next, scatter the chocolate pieces amongst the bananas and then spread the toffee sauce evenly all over the top using a hot palate knife. Spoon the mascarpone mixture over the top of this and spread it into the edges or flutes of the tin. To finish, grate a little more chocolate over the top. Leave in the fridge to set for at least 3 hours.

# Cherry and Almond Tart

A really good looking tart that is great served hot with custard or cold with oodles of clotted cream.

**SERVES 12**

375g sweet shortcrust pastry
350g jar stoned cherries (drained weight)
100g unsalted butter
100g caster sugar
3 medium free-range eggs, beaten
50g **Horlicks Original powder**
3 tablespoons milk
$\frac{1}{2}$ teaspoon almond extract
150g ground almonds

75g icing sugar, sifted
1 tablespoon flaked almonds

**You will need a 23x30cm greased loose-based baking tin and some baking beans**

Preheat the oven to 180°C/350°F/ Gas Mark 4.

Roll out the pastry and line the tin with it, trimming the edges. Prick the pastry with a fork a few times, then line with baking parchment and fill with baking beans. Blind-bake the pastry for 15 minutes, then remove the parchment and beans and bake for a further 10 minutes, until golden. Turn the oven down to 160°C/325°F/Gas Mark 3.

Let this cool slightly and then fill the base with the cherries. Put the butter and sugar into a bowl and beat for 2 minutes. Then add the eggs, Horlicks and milk, a little at a time, and beat with an electric whisk until pale and creamy. Now add the almond extract and fold in the ground almonds.

Pour the mixture over the cherries and spread it out with a spatula. Bake in the centre of the oven for 35–40 minutes until risen and golden. Remove from the oven and allow to cool a little.

Mix the icing sugar with a tablespoon of cold water and drizzle it over the tart in irregular lines. Sprinkle the flaked almonds over the top.

Remove from the tin and cut into 12 squares or slices.

### A MUG OF SOOTHING DIASTOID?

Hmmm, not quite got the same ring, has it? Not surprising then that when the Horlicks brothers William and James originally named their drink Diastoid, it didn't take them too long to figure that the family name might make for a better fit!

# Raspberry and Horlicks Crème Brûlée

Always a great favourite with pudding lovers but adding Horlicks gives this classic dish a real extra depth of flavour.

**MAKES 8 POTS**

### Horlicks HINTS

**If you have one (and wish to impress your guests!) a quick blast with a mini-blowtorch will caramelise the tops perfectly.**

6 medium free-range egg yolks
50g caster sugar
50g **Horlicks Original powder**
600ml single cream
200g raspberries (frozen are fine)
60g Demerara sugar

**You will need 8 ramekins or similar little pots for this recipe**

Preheat the oven to 150°C/300°F/ Gas Mark 2.

Put the egg yolks, sugar and Horlicks into a bowl and beat with a wooden spoon until thoroughly mixed. Next, heat the cream gently in a saucepan until nearly boiling and then pour this into the egg yolk mixture. Stir together well and then strain the creamy mixture into a large jug.

Divide the raspberries between the 8 ramekins and then pour equal amounts of the custard into each. Put the ramekins into a high-sided baking tin and add about an inch of water to the tin. Place in the centre of the oven and bake for 45 minutes or until the custard has just set. Remove and cool, then chill in the fridge until needed, but for at least one hour.

About an hour before you are ready to devour them, sprinkle the Demerara sugar evenly over each dish. Place them onto a baking tray under a hot grill to quickly brown them until the sugar has melted and just starts to bubble. Keep an eye on them, as this will happen quite quickly. Remove from the grill and as the sugar starts to cool it will crisp.

Leave for at least half an hour before serving.

# HORLICK'S MALTED MILK

## ALWAYS UP TO THE "STANDARD"

# Poached Pears with Horlicks Honey Custard

Horlicks honey custard is the star of this show with the delicious contrast of just-pink pears infused with cinnamon.

**SERVES 6**

**For the pears**
6 firm pears
4 tablespoons granulated sugar
5cm cinnamon stick
175ml red wine

**For the custard**
570ml milk
55ml double cream
$\frac{1}{2}$ teaspoon vanilla extract
4 egg yolks
30g caster sugar
1 tablespoon runny honey
1 tablespoon **Horlicks Original powder**
1 level tablespoon cornflour

Peel the pears, leaving the stalks attached, and place in a pan deep enough to contain the liquid that will cover the pears. Add the sugar, cinnamon and wine and then top up with water so as to just cover the pears. Bring gently to the boil and then simmer for 30 minutes or until the pears are tender. Remove them from the pan with a slotted spoon and set aside. Boil the remaining liquid until you have a syrup and pour this over the pears.

To make the custard, put the milk, cream and vanilla into a pan and bring gently to the boil. In a bowl whisk the egg yolks, sugar, honey, Horlicks and cornflour until blended. Pour the hot milk into the egg mixture and stir, then return it all to the pan to heat until thick and creamy.

Serve one pear per person with a jug of delicious Horlicks honey custard.

### ALWAYS UP TO THE STANDARD

*Opposite*: This little girl proudly waves the Royal Standard. Horlicks could justifiably claim to live up to that standard, not least because in 1914, a baronetcy was conferred upon James Horlick.

# White Chocolate Croissant Pudding

This is a gorgeous take on the traditional bread and butter pudding but much lighter and fluffier and with the added Horlicks your taste buds will bounce with delight.

**SERVES 8**

6 large butter croissants
   (preferably stale)
400ml milk
400ml double cream
1 teaspoon vanilla extract
3 medium free-range eggs
4 medium free-range egg yolks
150g caster sugar
50g **Horlicks Original powder**
150g white chocolate
icing sugar, to dust

**You will need an ovenproof dish roughly 25x30cm**

Preheat the oven to 180°C/350°F/Gas Mark 4.

Slice the croissants in half lengthways to give you a top and a base. Arrange the bases in the bottom of the dish and then the tops above them, cutting up the last top to fit in the gaps.

Put the milk, cream and vanilla into a pan and bring gently to the boil, then remove to cool slightly. Into a separate bowl crack all the eggs, then add the extra yolks, sugar and Horlicks and beat until pale and creamy.

Add the egg mixture to the pan of cream and break the chocolate into it. Heat gently until all the ingredients are mixed and the chocolate has completely melted. Pour this over the croissants, reserving a little to serve hot with the pudding.

Cover with foil and bake in the centre of the oven for 20–25 minutes until the egg custard has just set. Remove from the oven and allow to cool slightly. Dust with icing sugar and pop the dish under a hot grill for a few minutes to crisp.

# Pecan Toffee Ice Cream

**If you like ice cream you will just love this, it's deliciously creamy with the indulgent toffee sauce – food to make you feel good.**

**SERVES 4**

**For the toffee sauce**
100g butter
4 tablespoons Demerara sugar
1 teaspoon golden syrup
2 tablespoons **Horlicks Original powder**
3 tablespoons double cream

250ml milk
250ml double cream
4 egg yolks
100g caster sugar
50g pecan nuts, roughly chopped

To make the toffee sauce melt the butter in a saucepan, add the sugar and syrup and stir until dissolved. Then add the Horlicks and cream and stir until everything is well blended. Allow to cool.

Put the milk and cream into a saucepan and bring gently to the boil. Remove from the heat. In a separate bowl combine the egg yolks and sugar and beat until thick and creamy. Stir in the cooled toffee sauce and mix well, then pour in the creamy mixture. Return everything to the pan and heat gently, stirring all the time until the mixture thickens.

Allow to cool, stir in the pecans and then pour into a suitable freezer container. When cold, transfer to the freezer. After 2 hours, remove from the freezer and mix well with a fork. Return it to the freezer and repeat twice more. This will stop the ice cream crystallising. If you have a fast-freeze compartment these times can be reduced by half. Leave overnight and then your ice cream will be ready.

Bring out of the freezer 10 minutes before serving.

**MORE HIP HORLICKS**

When seeking to retire to chic lodgings, you might also be able to find a mug on the room service menus of some of the city's more glamorous hotels, Clerkenwell's uber-cool Zetter amongst them. (Just remember to hang the Do Not Disturb sign before you begin!)

# Strawberry French Toast

There is something special about eggy bread for a weekend breakfast. Just try this variation with fresh strawberries and Horlicks to take the flavour sensation to new heights.

**SERVES 4**

2 medium free-range eggs
50ml full-fat milk
1 tablespoon **Horlicks Original powder**
25g unsalted butter
4 thick slices stale rustic bread
1 tablespoon strawberry jam
300g strawberries, hulled and sliced
icing sugar, to dust

Put the eggs, milk and Horlicks into a flat dish and whisk the ingredients together with a fork. Don't worry if the Horlicks doesn't completely dissolve, as it will add to the final crispiness.

Gently heat the butter in a non-stick frying pan, dip the bread into the eggy mixture so that it is completely coated and fry gently for 2–3 minutes on each side until golden. Keep the toast warm and repeat with the rest of the bread.

In a separate pan, warm the jam with a tablespoon of water until melted and then add the strawberries. Heat gently for one minute and then divide between each slice of French toast. Serve on warm plates and dust the strawberry toast with icing sugar.

### FACTORY LIFE

*Opposite*: Pictures from the early-mid 20th century from the factory floor at Poges Lane. James Horlick had the factory built in 1906 and whilst the hot urns of water might have disappeared, the factory still produces Horlicks to this very day.

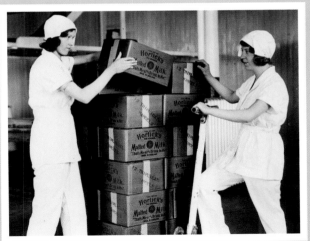

# Horlicks and Blueberry Muffins

A great comfort food completed and lifted by fresh blueberries, and the perfect partner to a morning cup of coffee.

**MAKES 12 MUFFINS**

120g butter
50g sugar
40g **Horlicks Original powder**
75ml full-fat milk
2 medium free-range eggs, beaten
150g plain flour
2 teaspoons baking powder
150g fresh blueberries

**You will need a greased muffin tray or 12 muffin cases**

Cream the butter, sugar and Horlicks together in a bowl and then gradually add the milk and eggs. Mix well for 2–3 minutes. Your mixture may look a little like scrambled eggs, but don't worry. Sieve in the flour and baking powder and stir the whole mixture to combine. The mixture will now be fairly stiff. Chill for one hour.

Preheat the oven to 180°C/350°F/ Gas Mark 4.

Put a spoonful of mixture into each muffin case so that they are about half full. Stud the tops with the blueberries, roughly divided into 12 depending on size, and then bake in the centre of the oven for 20 minutes or until well risen and golden.

Allow to cool slightly before serving warm.

**Horlicks HINTS**

**These muffins taste every bit as delicious with different fruits. Try making them with raspberries or cranberries.**

# Horlicks Smoked Chicken and Mushroom Risotto

With a strong Italian heritage, this dish is full of exciting flavour. Risotto, meaning 'little rice', absorbs all the flavours and the Horlicks definitely adds to its delicious creamy texture.

**SERVES 2**

50g butter
$1/_2$ medium onion, finely diced
1 teaspoon fresh thyme leaves
1 clove of garlic, finely diced
150g Arborio rice
2 tablespoons **Horlicks Original powder**
500ml chicken stock
50g smoked cooked chicken, cut into thin strips
3 mushrooms, sliced
1 tablespoon double cream

Melt the butter in a wide-based pan then add in the onion, thyme, garlic and rice and gently sweat until the rice starts to go clear, stirring all the time.

Add in the Horlicks and stir thoroughly. Add in the stock a splash at a time allowing for the rice to soak it up before adding more. This will take about 10 minutes.

Once most of the stock is added, taste the rice to see if it is cooked (risotto rice should be cooked *al dente*, which means firm but not hard). If it's not quite cooked, keep adding more stock.

Once the rice is cooked add the chicken, mushrooms and cream and stir until the rice absorbs about 60% of the liquid. Finish with freshly chopped parsley and serve.

## HORLICKS AROUND THE WORLD

In the Philippines, Horlicks is sold as a sweet in packets of chocolate-flavoured discs. In India – the world's largest consumer of Horlicks since 1975 – it is made with buffalo milk. Around 20 million cups of Horlicks are drunk in India every year!

# Horlicks, Cheese and Leek Crumble

**Savoury crumbles are few and far between. This easy recipe is comfort food with a capital 'C' – you'll just adore it.**

**For the cheese sauce**
50g butter
65g plain flour
350ml full-fat milk
2 tablespoon **Horlicks Original powder**
100g mature Cheddar, grated
$\frac{1}{2}$ teaspoon English mustard
black pepper
500g leeks, trimmed and sliced into 2cm rings

**For the crumble topping**
275g plain flour
150g butter, cut into cubes
35g Parmesan, finely grated
1 teaspoon mixed dried herbs
salt and pepper

Preheat the oven to 180°C/350°F/ Gas Mark 4.

First make the cheese sauce. Melt the butter in a pan, then gradually add the flour, stirring constantly until it becomes smooth and a light nutty brown colour. Add the milk gradually and then whisk in the Horlicks. Stir until hot and thickened. Add in the cheese, English mustard and a good grind of black pepper. When the cheese has melted, remove the pan from the heat and lay a piece of clingfilm on the surface of the sauce to avoid a skin forming. Next, steam the leeks until just tender.

Meanwhile, to make the crumble topping, sieve the flour into a bowl. Add the cubes of butter and rub them into the flour until you have the texture of breadcrumbs. Stir in the Parmesan and the herbs.

Tip the cooked leeks into a suitable baking dish, season and pour the cheese sauce over. Cover with the crumble mixture and bake in the centre of the oven for 30 minutes until the crumble surface turns a light golden brown.

Allow to cool a little before serving on its own or with a few crispy potato wedges.

# Horlicks Chocolate Mousse

A fine finish to any meal. This yummy rich dessert will go down a storm with kids of all ages!

**MAKES 6–8 PORTIONS**

300g plain chocolate
30g unsalted butter
2 tablespoons **Horlicks Original powder**
6 medium free-range eggs
2 tablespoons caster sugar
6 fresh or ready-to-eat dried apricots, sliced into thin slices

**You will need 6 ramekins or 8 demitasse coffee cups**

Break the chocolate into pieces in a bowl, add the butter and Horlicks and microwave for 3–4 minutes or until all the ingredients have melted. This can alternatively be done by placing the bowl over a pan of boiling water. Leave to cool.

Separate the eggs and put the yolks and sugar into one bowl and whisk the egg whites in another bowl until you have stiff peaks. Mix the chocolate with the egg yolks and sugar, until thoroughly combined. Add a quarter of the egg whites to the chocolate and beat and then fold in the remainder of the whites, a little at a time and mixing very gently, until they are thoroughly mixed together.

Pour the mixture into ramekins or demitasse cups. Place them on a tray, cover with clingfilm and refrigerate for 4 hours.

Serve decorated with the slices of apricot.

**Horlicks HINTS**

**You can serve these with crisp biscuits or wafers for a nice crunch against the smooth, silky texture of the mousse.**

# Bacon and Broccoli Pasta Carbonara

**A truly delicious quick and easy dish packed with great flavours of smoked bacon and Pecorino and that maltiness to wrap around the pasta.**

**SERVES 2**

200g smoked streaky bacon, diced
3 medium free-range eggs
100ml double cream
2 tablespoons **Horlicks Original powder**
freshly ground black pepper
4 tablespoons Pecorino cheese, finely grated (Parmesan will also work fine)
225g dried spaghetti
olive oil
100g broccoli, broken into tiny florets
a small handful of parsley, chopped

Fry the diced bacon in a dry pan until crispy. Remove onto kitchen paper to drain and set aside.

Whisk together the eggs, cream and Horlicks until there are no grains of Horlicks remaining. Season with black pepper and add all but a couple of teaspoons of the Pecorino cheese.

Cook the pasta in boiling salted water with a little olive oil for eight minutes and then add in the broccoli florets. Cook for two more minutes until the pasta is just *al dente*.

This next part needs to be done quickly. Drain the pasta and broccoli in a colander and immediately return it to the pan so there is a little moisture on it. Add in the egg mixture and the bacon and stir well. The eggs will then proceed to cook in the hot, moist pasta. Tip into warm pasta bowls, scatter with parsley and the reserved Pecorino and serve.

## ONE OF THE OLDEST RECIPES AROUND...

The recipe has remained the same since James Horlicks first produced Horlicks Malted Milk back in 1883. That means it's been around longer than the teabag (invented 1904) and the cornflake (invented 1906)!

# Roast Pheasant on Sautéed Pears with Horlicks Bread Sauce

Bread sauce is a traditional but rather bland sauce, which has lost favour with today's gourmets. The slight sweetness of Horlicks enhances and reinvigorates a simple recipe, and is especially good with game and rich meat dishes.

**SERVES 2**

**For the pheasant**
1 plump young pheasant
vegetable oil
4 streaky bacon rashers
500ml chicken stock
salt and freshly ground black pepper

**For the bread sauce**
1 small onion, peeled
4 whole cloves
300ml full-fat milk
50g fresh white breadcrumbs
1 tablespoon **Horlicks Original powder**
1 tablespoon double cream
cayenne pepper
salt

**For the pears**
25g butter
1 firm pear, cored and sliced
1 tablespoon Demerara sugar

Preheat the oven to 200°C/400°F/ Gas Mark 6.

Wipe the pheasant with a clean, damp cloth to remove any stray feathers. Brush it all over with vegetable oil and season with salt and pepper. Stretch the bacon rashers with the blunt edge of a knife and wrap them over the top of the bird.

Put the pheasant on a rack in a roasting tin and pour the stock into the tin (this will help to keep it moist). Roast for 30 minutes, basting occasionally and then remove the bacon to brown the skin of the pheasant (if you like, you can roll up the bacon rashers, thread them on a skewer and leave in the roasting tin to serve with the pheasant once cooked). Cook for a further 10 minutes until the bird is tender and the juices run clear when pierced with a skewer.

While the pheasant is roasting you can make the bread sauce. Take the peeled onion, leave it whole but stud it with the cloves. Put it into a saucepan with the milk and heat very gently for 10 minutes, allowing the onion to infuse the milk. Remove the onion, add the breadcrumbs and Horlicks and cook gently, stirring occasionally, until you have the consistency of thick porridge. Season with a little salt and cayenne pepper, stir in the cream and your bread sauce is ready.

Melt the butter in a small frying pan and add the pears and sugar and sauté until golden. Arrange the slices on a serving dish with the pheasant cut into 4 portions on top and serve with a dish of warm bread sauce.

# West Country Pork in Cider Sauce

Picture the scene: friends around the dinner table supping gently on their mugs of cider as they devour this tender pork doused with a truly exemplary sauce.

## SERVES 4

### For the pork
1 pork tenderloin, approximately 500g
vegetable oil, for frying
1 sweet eating apple, cored and sliced

### For the cider sauce
1 tablespoon shallots, finely diced
knob of butter
1 tablespoon plain flour
1 tablespoon **Horlicks Original powder**
100ml medium cider
50ml double cream
salt and freshly ground black pepper

Preheat the oven to 180°C/350°F/Gas Mark 4.

Using a sharp knife, trim off any fat or sinew from the pork tenderloin. Heat a little oil in a frying pan, add the tenderloin in two halves to fit into the pan and brown the meat all over for about 2 minutes. Transfer the tenderloin to an oven dish and roast in the oven for 30 minutes. After 20 minutes of cooking time, add the apple slices to the roasting tray.

While the pork is roasting, make the cider sauce. Sweat off the shallots in a pan with a knob of butter until they are translucent. Remove the pan from the heat and stir in the flour and Horlicks with a splash of the cider. Mix into a paste (a *roux*), return to the heat and then gradually add the remaining cider, cooking over a gentle heat and stirring all the time to avoid any lumps. Finish by adding the cream and seasoning with salt and plenty of pepper.

When the tenderloin is cooked remove it from the oven and leave to rest for 5 minutes. Slice into medallions and divide between four warm plates with slices of apple in between. Spoon over the creamy sauce and serve.

### Horlicks HINTS

You can serve this with a number of accompaniments. Some new potatoes and a simple rocket salad is simple and effective.

# South African Multi-Seed Bread

This is a substantial multiseed loaf bursting with flavour and goodness. Try it with both sweet and savoury toppings.

125g wholemeal bread flour
150g strong white bread flour
1 level tablespoon baking powder
100g multigrain porridge
1 level teaspoon salt
3 tablespoons **Horlicks Original powder**
45g golden linseeds
30g white poppy seeds
30g pumpkin seeds
30g sesame seeds
30g sunflower seeds
10g nigella (onion) seeds
40g baby pine nuts
250g tub Greek-style yoghurt
2 tablespoons runny honey
2 tablespoons mild/medium olive oil
100ml semi-skimmed milk

**You will need a 900g loaf tin, well greased, and some baking parchment**

Heat the oven to 180°C/350°F/ Gas Mark 4.

In a bowl mix all the dry ingredients, seeds and nuts together with a wooden spoon. It's really important to make sure they are combined well otherwise you will have an unbalanced final loaf.

Now add the rest of the ingredients and mix until you have a sticky dough that slides slowly off the spoon.

Line the base of the tin with baking parchment and spoon the dough into the tin, finishing with a flourish of all the seeds on the top.

Place the tin in the centre of the oven for 20 minutes then reduce the heat to 150°C/300°F/Gas Mark 2 for a further 20 minutes.

Slide a kitchen knife into the loaf and if the knife comes out clean then the bread is cooked, if not, cook for a further 10 minutes. Leave to cool before turning out.

## SETTING UP SCHOOL

In 1928, the William Horlick High School in Racine, Wisconsin, USA, opened its doors to students for the first time. The school was named in William's honour – he had donated the land ten years earlier. The school is still in operation today.

# Kedgeree

A real classic from the days of the Raj. Adding Horlicks to the cooking liquor enhances this fantastic breakfast dish beyond belief.

**SERVES 4**

500g natural smoked haddock
   fillets
300ml semi-skimmed milk
2 tablespoons **Horlicks Original
   powder**
50g butter
1 medium onion, diced
2 teaspoons medium curry powder
$\frac{1}{2}$ teaspoon turmeric
225g basmati rice, washed
4 free-range eggs, hard-boiled
2 tablespoons parsley, chopped
1 tablespoon lemon juice
1 lemon, cut into 8 wedges
1 tablespoon fresh chives,
   chopped
salt and freshly ground black
   pepper

First, place the haddock fillets in a large frying pan and cover with the milk and Horlicks. Bring to a simmer and leave to cook for about 10 minutes. Remove the haddock, and keep it warm in the oven. Retain the liquid – this is very important.

Now melt half the butter and sauté the onions until transparent and then add the curry powder and turmeric. Turn up the heat and add the washed rice, stir once and now add the liquid reserved from the fish. Stir once again, cover the pan, turn the heat down to 'low' and leave with a lid on for exactly 15 minutes.

In the meantime, remove the fish skin and any bones and flake the fish. Take 2 of the boiled eggs and chop them.

After 15 minutes remove the lid from the pan, fluff up the rice, add the flaked smoked haddock, the remaining butter, the parsley, the two chopped eggs, the salt and pepper and the lemon juice. Mix gently together. Turn the heat off and cover the pan with a clean tea towel for 5 minutes. This helps to draw off excess liquid.

Serve immediately onto warm plates, garnish with a wedge of lemon, the other two sliced boiled eggs, a sprinkle of chopped chives and a tablespoon of Indian mango chutney.

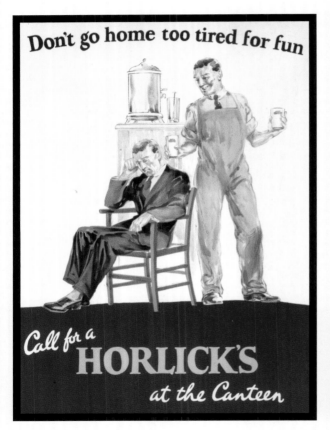

# Malted Lamb with Noodles

Cooking in a wok is just such fun. Lamb and lemon is a magic combination and this dish proves the point. It's easy to prepare in advance and quick to cook – its wokalicious!

**SERVES 4 PEOPLE**

1kg English lamb neck fillet, diced
    into 1cm slices
2 tablespoons **Horlicks Original
    powder**
2 tablespoons rice flour
2 tablespoons breadcrumbs
1 tablespoon cumin
1 teaspoon dried rosemary
$\frac{1}{2}$ teaspoon salt
good grind of black pepper
sesame oil, for frying
1 lemon, cut into 8 wedges
250g crispy noodles
50g crushed peanuts

**This is best cooked in a wok**

Place the lamb in a bowl and sprinkle over the Horlicks, rice flour, breadcrumbs, cumin, rosemary, salt and pepper. Mix it all together to thoroughly coat the lamb and leave in a cool place to marinate for at least 1 hour.

Heat the oil in the wok and cook the lemon wedges for 2 minutes.

Add the lamb and fry until golden. Remove the lamb and the lemons with a slotted spoon and drain onto kitchen paper.

Meanwhile, shallow-fry the noodles in the wok and remaining juices until crispy.

Present the crispy noodles on serving plates, spoon over the lamb mixture and sprinkle with the crushed peanuts.

## CANTEEN LIFE

*Opposite*: Over 130 years and through two World Wars, Horlicks became a staple of the workplace, the school and thousands of industrial organizations where communal feeding took place. Horlicks was sold as a 'complete and well balanced nourishment'.

# Horlicks and Vanilla Bavarois

This delicious dessert, colloquially known as Bavarian set cream, will really impress your friends. Presented with fresh strawberries and grated chocolate, your guests will want to vote you the best cook ever.

**SERVES 4**

6 leaves gelatine
150ml double cream
2 medium free-range eggs, yolks
   and whites separated
2 tablespoons **Horlicks Original
   powder**
25g caster sugar
350ml full-fat milk
$\frac{1}{2}$ teaspoon vanilla essence

16 strawberries, hulled, to serve
4 tablepsoons Chantilly cream,
   to serve
dark chocolate, for grating,
   to serve

**You'll need 4 x 100ml dariole
moulds (easy to find in most
cookware sections)**

Soak the gelatine in cold water until soft and pliable.

Whip the cream into soft peaks, and whip the egg whites into stiff peaks in separate bowls. In a third bowl, whisk the Horlicks, sugar, and egg yolks together until light and creamy.

Pour the milk into a saucepan, add the vanilla and bring to the boil. Remove from the heat for 10 seconds, allowing to settle, and then slowly add it to the egg yolk mixture, stirring constantly. Now put this mixture back into a clean heavy-based pan on a very low heat stirring again (it must not boil!). After the mixture has thickened slightly, remove from the heat and add the gelatine leaves and stir until dissolved. Strain the whole lot into a bowl using a sieve and leave to cool.

Once cool, fold in the whites and the cream, pour into moulds and set in the fridge for 1 hour. Remove the Bavarois from the moulds by sitting the moulds in warm water for a few seconds, then shaking them out onto the plate.

Serve with sliced fresh strawberries, a spoon of Chantilly cream and grated dark chocolate.

## Horlicks HINTS

To separate eggs, crack your egg over a glass bowl. Turn it upright and gently open the shell into two halves, keeping the egg in the lower half. Pour the egg from one half into the other, letting the egg white fall into the bowl, but keeping the yolk intact in the shell halves as you pour, until only the yolk remains.

# Methi Gosht
# (Creamy Lamb Curry with Fenugreek)

You'll love the lightly bitter,
but still sweet and fragrant
taste of the fenugreek mingling
with the spicy braised lamb.
An irresistible dish.

**SERVES 4–6**

**For the marinade**
1 teaspoon salt
$1/_2$ teaspoon turmeric
1 teaspoon cumin seeds
2 teaspoons coriander seeds
$1/_2$ teaspoon fenugreek seeds
8 large cloves garlic
1 small red onion, roughly chopped
4 fresh green Thai chillies
2cm cube fresh ginger, sliced
3 tablespoons **Horlicks Original powder**
200ml Greek-style natural yoghurt

1kg shoulder of lamb, diced into 3cm cubes
2 tablespoons ghee or vegetable oil
2 medium red onions, peeled and thinly sliced
2 good handfuls dried fenugreek leaves
450g baby new potatoes, cooked and halved
100ml double cream

2 tablespoons freshly chopped coriander, to garnish
lime wedges, to garnish

To make the marinade, put all the ingredients except the Greek yoghurt into a pestle and mortar or blender, and grind or blitz into a paste. Stir in 100ml of the yoghurt to make a thick, deliciously scented marinade. Put the lamb into a bowl, add the yoghurt mixture, cover and leave to marinate for at least an hour. You can also cover it and put it in the fridge to marinate overnight if you wish.

Heat the ghee or oil in a heavy-based pan. Add the sliced onion and cook, stirring, until the onion is just golden. Add the lamb with all the marinade and cook, stirring, until it browns lightly. Add the fenugreek and 200ml of water. Bring to a boil, then turn down the heat and simmer for 1 hour or until the lamb is tender.

Add the potatoes and check to see how thick or thin the sauce is. If it is too thin, turn the heat up to high, bring to a boil and cook off the excess liquid. If it is too thick, add a bit of water and simmer for 5 minutes to finish cooking.

Finally, add the cream and remaining yoghurt and stir to mix. Simmer for a couple of minutes to heat through, and then serve over plain basmati rice, and garnish with coriander and some lime wedges.

**FIRST PRIZE!**

This 20th Century advert illustrates the real winning element behind Horlicks Malted Milk!

# Devilled Kidneys

There are as many ways to make this traditional favourite as there are roads to Rome. This is a great, tried and tested recipe for perfect devilled kidneys for breakfast or supper.

**SERVES 4**

100ml double cream
1 level teaspoon English mustard powder
1 tablespoon **Horlicks Original powder**
1 tablespoon Worcestershire sauce
$1/_2$ teaspoon cayenne pepper
12 lambs' kidneys
25g unsalted butter
freshly chopped parsley, to serve

In a small bowl, mix together the cream, mustard, Horlicks, Worcestershire sauce, and cayenne pepper (a whisk will help disperse the powders).

Snip out the white core of each kidney with a sharp pair of scissors and remove any skin. Cut each kidney into three. Melt the butter in a frying pan and, when sizzling, slide in the kidneys. Toss the kidneys in the butter for 3–4 minutes and then add the spicy, creamy mixture. Keep tossing the whole dish for 2 more minutes until the kidneys are coated in the rich sauce.

Kidneys cook quickly; when ready they will still have a hint of pink in the centre. Finish the dish with the chopped parsley.

**Horlicks HINTS**

**This classic is wonderful served on their own, on toasted triangles of wholemeal bread or on a lovely bed of fluffy basmati rice. Whatever way you go, scatter with freshly chopped parsley to finish.**

# THE HEALTH ALPHABET.

PRICE THREE PENCE

PUBLISHED BY
HORLICK'S MALTED MILK CO
SLOUGH, BUCKS, ENGLAND.

COPYRIGHT

# Scallops on Creamed Cabbage

King scallops with their firm texture and delicate flavour resting on tender cabbage that's been cooked with Horlicks and bacon makes this a meal that you won't ever want to end.

**SERVES 4**

**For the creamed cabbage**
1 tablespoon oil
25g butter
1 small clove of garlic, crushed
$1/_2$ onion, finely chopped
2 rashers smoked bacon or
   pancetta, diced
$1/_2$ Savoy cabbage, thick stalks
   removed and finely shredded
1 tablespoon **Horlicks Original
   powder**
100ml crème fraîche
1 tablespoon fresh parsley, chopped
salt and pepper

**For the scallops**
a little butter for frying
12 fresh King scallops
freshly ground black pepper
$1/_2$ lemon

To make the creamed cabbage, heat the oil and butter in a large pan and add the garlic, onion and bacon. Cover and fry gently until soft. Add the cabbage and cook gently, covered, until the cabbage begins to soften. Next, stir the Horlicks and crème fraîche into the cabbage. Bubble gently until the cabbage is cooked through. Taste and, if necessary, lightly season with salt and black pepper. Finally, scatter in the parsley. Keep warm while you prepare the scallops.

If you have a griddle use it here, lightly greased, otherwise melt the butter in a large frying pan until sizzling and slide in the scallops. Cook for two minutes on each side so that they are just firm to the touch (overcooked and they will become rubbery). Season with black pepper and squeeze the juice of half a lemon all over them while still in the pan.

Arrange the creamy cabbage on the plates and serve 3 scallops on top of each followed by any juices remaining in the pan.

**Horlicks HINTS**

Serve this exquisite little dish with a big thick chunk of crusty white bread and a nice glass of chilled white wine.

# Roasted Sausages and Onion with Sweet Mustard Sauce

Horlicks and wholegrain mustard make a great marriage when spooned over honey-roasted sausages and sweet red onions.

**SERVES 4**

2 large red onions, peeled and cut into eight
olive oil
a few sprigs fresh thyme
a good pinch of sugar
salt and black pepper
8 local butchers' handmade pork sausages
runny honey, for brushing

**For the sauce**
vegetable oil, for frying
1 tablespoon shallots, finely diced
4 tablespoons double cream
2 teaspoons wholegrain mustard
1 teaspoon honey
1 tablespoon **Horlicks Original powder**
salt and pepper

Preheat the oven to 180°C/350°F/ Gas Mark 4.

Lay the onions into a roasting tray and drizzle with olive oil, then scatter over the thyme, add a good pinch of sugar and season with plenty of salt and pepper.

Brush the sausages all over with honey and then nestle them amongst the onions in the roasting tray. Roast in the oven for 30 minutes or until the sausages are golden and cooked through and the onions are just crispy at the edges.

While they are cooking, make the lovely sweet mustard sauce. Put a splash of oil into a small pan, add the shallots and cook them off gently until translucent. Now add the cream, mustard, honey and Horlicks, taste and season and stir to combine.

Serve the sausages and onions dowsed in the sweet mustard sauce with some fluffy mash or crispy garlic potato wedges.

### AS EASY AS ABC

*Opposite*: The ABC of Horlicks. This beautiful illustration from the early 20th century seemed to make elementary sense. It was the nourishing drink that could help to keep you healthy, wise and well... for 'infants, invalids, the aged and travellers'.

# THE · HEALTH · ·ALPHABET·

This is the tale of A to Z - - - -
(A wonderful tale to tell)- - - - -
Of the drink that they drank. and
- - - - - - the food that they fed
To be wealthy and wise and well. -

# Smoked Trout with Malted Horseradish Sauce

Smoked trout will quiver with excitement as you combine the freshly grated horseradish, Horlicks and soured cream into a deliciously creamy sauce with a good spicy kick.

**SERVES 4**

**For the horseradish sauce**
5 heaped teaspoons freshly grated horseradish (take care when grating – the aroma is quite fierce!)
$1/_2$ teaspoon English mustard powder
1 heaped teaspoon **Horlicks Original powder**
1 tablespoon sour cream
1 teaspoon lemon juice
a good pinch salt

dressed mixed rocket and watercress leaves
500g cold smoked trout
4 wedges of lemon
black pepper to serve

To make the creamed horseradish mix all of the sauce ingredients together in a small dish. This is best done about an hour in advance to let the flavours fuse together.

Arrange the rocket and watercress on plates and the smoked trout on the top in curls or waves. Add a dollop of the horseradish sauce, a wedge of lemon and grind plenty of black pepper over the top. Serve with crusty bread.

# Malted Mocha Coffee Milkshake

There is little better on a summer's day than a tall glass of iced coffee to keep you cool. Here we take it one step further by adding malty Horlicks and chocolate.

**SERVES 4**

1 tablespoon instant coffee
1 tablespoon drinking chocolate
   powder
1 tablespoon **Horlicks Original**
   **powder**
1 tablespoon maple syrup
4 scoops vanilla ice cream
1 litre milk

**You'll need a blender and 4 tall drinking glasses**

Put all the ingredients into a blender and whiz for 30 seconds.

Pour into the tall glasses, add a couple of straws and serve.

## MALTED MILK OF THE FUTURE!

Back in the 1950s, Horlicks were the sponsors of the radio programme, 'The Adventures of Dan Dare, Pilot of the Future', which broadcast on Radio Luxembourg. The 'Horlicks Spacemen's Club' was established to coincide with the broadcasts.

# Deep-fried Salmon Goujons

You'll be amazed at how great the Horlicks is in the batter; it makes it light, fluffy and extra crispy, wrapped around the soft, succulent salmon pieces.

**SERVES 6**

400g plain flour
salt and freshly ground black
   pepper
4 heaped tablespoons **Horlicks
   Original powder**
400ml ice cold sparkling water
600g salmon, cut into finger-sized
   strips (about 8cm long)
lemon wedges

Put 200g of the flour in a bowl and season with salt and pepper.

Into a separate bowl sieve the remaining flour, add the Horlicks and the water (important that it is cold and fresh for best results) then whisk until smooth.

Dip the salmon into the bowl of seasoned flour and wrap around to give each piece a good coating, then shake off the excess flour and dip them into the batter bowl, one at a time. Then, a few at a time dip them into a hot deep-fat fryer (190°C) using kitchen tongs to hold half in the oil until it starts to float (this is important so they do not sink and stick to the bottom). Wait a few minutes until golden brown, turning if necessary. Remove from the oil with a slotted spoon and place onto kitchen paper to drain.

**Horlicks HINTS**

These taste great served with a handful of mixed leaves, a good squeeze of lemon juice and a nice dollop of homemade tartare sauce.

**"** *It's just as I said on television the other night*—you need a good blaze this time of year. And a good hot drink last thing.

I mean a *real* drink. Horlicks: that's the stuff. A good creamy cupful, Horlicks is. Sends you off to sleep really warm and comfortable.

There's nothing like a good night's sleep for keeping up your health and strength.

Try Horlicks yourself. You'll soon feel the benefit. **"**

*The food-drink of the night*

13

# Roast Fennel and Pistachio Salad

Fennel coated with Horlicks and breadcrumbs and scattered with whole pistachio nuts on a bed of mixed leaves is the perfect dish for ladies who lunch, darling.

**SERVES 4**

4 small fennel bulbs (about 150g each), stalks trimmed almost back to the bulb, slightly trimmed at base and each bulb cut lengthways into four
olive oil, for drizzling
100g fresh white breadcrumbs
2 tablespoons **Horlicks Original powder**
1 heaped teaspoon dried mixed herbs
mixed dressed salad leaves
50g shelled pistachio nuts
salt and freshly ground black pepper

Preheat the oven to 180°C/350°F/Gas Mark 4.

Put the fennel into a roasting tin and drizzle them with olive oil. Take each piece and, with your hands, make sure each is completely coated with the oil.

Put the breadcrumbs, Horlicks and herbs into a flat dish and season really well with salt and plenty of black pepper. Mix together well and dip the fennel segments into the breadcrumb mixture, making sure they are completely coated. Pop them back into the roasting pan, drizzle with a little more oil and roast in the oven for 30 minutes or until a sharp knife pierced through shows they are really tender and the coating is crispy and golden. Remove from the oven and allow to cool a little.

Put a good handful of mixed dressed salad leaves on each plate, arrange four segments of crispy fennel over the top of each and scatter with pistachio nuts. Serve with some crispy ciabatta bread.

# Coconut and Minced Pork Kofte

A delicious teasing taste of Horlicks, coconut and minced pork spiced with cumin served in a crispy lettuce shell.

**SERVES 4 AS A STARTER OR LUNCH**

400g minced pork
1 medium onion, grated
1 tablespoon desiccated coconut
1 tablespoon **Horlicks Original powder**
1 teaspoon ground cumin
1 teaspoon chopped fresh parsley
1 teaspoon chopped fresh coriander (plus extra for garnish)
3 tablespoons fresh white breadcrumbs
salt and freshly ground black pepper
sesame or vegetable oil, for frying

1 medium carrot, grated
1 tablespoon sweet chilli dipping sauce
4 crispy lettuce leaf 'shells' (Cos or Romaine are ideal)

Put the pork, onion, coconut, Horlicks and cumin into a bowl and mix together with your hands. Then add the herbs, breadcrumbs, plenty of salt and pepper and mix thoroughly.

Divide the mixture roughly into 8 and squeeze each into a ball, then gradually roll out into a sausage shape between the palms of your hands (having wet hands makes this process easier as the pork will not stick to them as much). Lay each kofte on a tray lined with greaseproof paper and chill them in the fridge for at least 4 hours or, better still, overnight.

Heat some oil in a frying pan and gently fry the kofte for 10 minutes until thoroughly cooked through and golden on the outside.

In a small bowl, mix together the grated carrot and chilli sauce. Lay out four lettuce shells, put 1 or 2 koftes onto each, spoon over some chilli sauce and scatter with the remaining coriander.

## Horlicks HINTS

Be sure to wet your hands before trying to form the sausage shapes. It will make the process much easier, ensuring they don't stick quite so much.

# Wild Mushroom Soup

This silky and seductive soup is infused with Horlicks, nutmeg and Madeira, making it the absolute king of mushroom soups.

**SERVES 4**

50g unsalted butter
100g shallots, diced
450g wild mushrooms
a pinch ground nutmeg
salt and freshly ground black
    pepper
600ml vegetable stock
$1\frac{1}{2}$ tablespoons **Horlicks Original powder**
1 tablespoon Madeira wine

Melt the butter in a large pan, add the shallots and sauté them gently for 3–4 minutes without browning them. Break up the mushrooms by hand and add them to the pan with the nutmeg, a good pinch of salt and plenty of black pepper and sauté for five minutes. Add the vegetable stock, Horlicks and the Madeira and simmer for 20 minutes.

Remove from the heat and allow to cool a little and then add 200ml of cold water and blitz until silky smooth. Reheat gently when you are ready to serve.

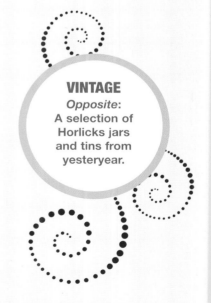

**VINTAGE**
*Opposite*:
A selection of Horlicks jars and tins from yesteryear.

# Chilli- and Thyme-Roasted Root Vegetables

This is a great way to turn everyday vegetables into a special occasion treat. The Horlicks makes the coating extra crispy and packs in the flavour.

1 small swede, cut into 2cm chunks
1 large onion, cut into 2cm chunks
2 large potatoes, cut into 2cm chunks
2 medium carrots, skin on, cut into 1cm rounds
2 cloves of garlic
2 tablespoons **Horlicks Original powder**
2 level teaspoons chilli powder
50g butter
4 tablespoons sunflower oil
1 tablespoon fresh thyme leaves
salt and black pepper

Pre heat the oven to 220°C/425°F/ Gas Mark 7.

Put all the vegetables, except the onions, into a pan of cold, lightly salted water and bring to the boil. Simmer for about 8 minutes until slightly softened and then drain. Next, finely chop the garlic and mix together in a small bowl with the Horlicks and chilli powder.

Pop the butter and the oil in a roasting tray, add the onions and then place the tray over a hot hob, allowing the butter to foam (hold the tray with a cloth at a slant). Reduce the heat and add the Horlicks mixture to the tray, mix well then add the remaining vegetables.

Mix all the vegetables together in the roasting tray to cover them all in the juices and remove from the heat. Add the thyme and season generously with salt and pepper. Toss once more and then roast in the oven for about 45–50 minutes until golden and crispy.

This makes the perfect vegetable accompaniment to steak, chicken or pork.

### THE FOOD DRINK OF THE NIGHT

Opposite: Horlicks has always been the perfect drink to wind down with as the day draws to a close. This 1960s advert declared it the perfect night-time nourishment.

# Veal Fricassée

Combined in this classic supper dish are mace and Horlicks, which kicks real flavour into a meal that virtually cooks itself.

**SERVES 4**

750g veal (you can use free-range chicken instead if you prefer)
salt and white pepper
50g butter
1 large onion, quartered
1 clove of garlic, diced
2 tablespoons plain flour
100ml dry white wine
2 tablespoons **Horlicks Original powder**
$\frac{1}{2}$ teaspoon fresh thyme leaves
1 tablespoon parsley, chopped
a good pinch of mace
2 bay leaves
8 small onions, peeled and boiled whole
8 button mushrooms, sautéed and cooled
100ml double cream

Cut the veal into 2cm cubes and season well with salt and pepper.

In a heavy-based pan melt the butter over a medium heat and cook the veal cubes for 2–3 minutes – they shouldn't be allowed to brown – just to seal in the juices. Now add the onions and garlic and cook for another 2 minutes. Stir in the flour to make the beginnings of a thick sauce. Pour in the wine, sprinkle in the Horlicks, adding the thyme, parsley, mace and bay leaves and bring to a simmer for between 45 minutes and 1 hour, until the veal is tender.

With a slotted spoon, remove only the veal and set aside, strain the remaining liquid disgarding everything else.

Return the strained sauce to the pan and add the veal, baby onions and the mushrooms and cook for a further 10 minutes. Now add the cream, stirring all the time until the sauce thickens.

Serve with hand-cut crispy sautéed potatoes and a shower of chopped parsley.

**MALTED MOUNTAINS...**
Did you know that there is a range of mountains in the Antarctic, named after everyone's favourite malted drink? Two expeditions, between 1933 and 1935, one led by Kennett L. Rawson and the other by Quin Blackburn identified the range.

# Thai-Style Crab Cakes

These are served hot and spicy with a definitive malty tang for a sumptuous and tastebud-tingling light lunch or dinner party starter.

**SERVES 4**

3 large potatoes, cut into
   10–12 cubes
3 tablespoons **Horlicks Original powder**
50g butter
3 small red chillies, finely diced
6 spring onions, finely diced
50g coriander, finely chopped
200g white crab meat
200g brown crab meat
2 medium free-range eggs, lightly beaten
2 teaspoons Thai fish sauce
200g breadcrumbs made from stale bread
vegetable oil, for frying
salt and pepper

Place the cubed potato into a pan, just about cover with water, add a pinch of salt and – here's the clever bit – spoon the Horlicks into the potato water and boil until they are soft. Drain, add the butter and mash until silky smooth. Leave to cool.

Place the chillies, spring onions and coriander into a large bowl with the crab meat, the two lightly-beaten eggs and the Thai fish sauce. Spoon in the mashed potato and combine all the ingredients well. Using your hands (it's the only way), form the mixture into fish cakes and roll each one in fresh breadcrumbs. These are traditionally round but try a square or triangular shape for fun. Place the fish cakes onto a lightly oiled platter and refrigerate for at least one hour.

Cook gently in hot oil in a frying pan until golden brown.

Serve on a bed of mixed leaves with a spiced-up cucumber salad or oodles of sweet chilli dipping sauce. If there are any cakes remaining, simply wrap them in clingfilm and freeze to enjoy at a later date.

### Horlicks HINTS

**Breadcrumbs freeze really well. Take advantage by tearing any stale bread into chunks, whizzing briefly in a food processor and storing into an airtight container in the freezer for when you need them.**

# Chilled Avocado and Watercress Soup

We always expect soup to be piping hot but this cool and refreshing soup will change your thinking. Its full of flavour and goodness and the trick is to prepare it in advance ready for your guests.

**SERVES 4**

1 scant tablespoon olive oil
1 medium onion, finely diced
700ml vegetable stock
1 tablespoon **Horlicks Original powder**
100g watercress, including trimmed stems, plus a little extra for garnish
1 large or 2 small avocados
3 tablespoons lime juice
salt and pepper
Cucumber slices for serving

**You'll also need a handful of ice cubes at the ready**

Heat the oil in a pan and cook the onion with a pinch of salt for 5 minutes until softened. Add the stock and Horlicks and bring up to the boil for 1 minute.

Remove from the heat and toss in the watercress, stir it in thoroughly and then add a handful of ice cubes to stop the cooking process and help retain the lush green colour. Season with salt and pepper and blitz until smooth. Pour into a bowl and chill in the fridge.

When chilled return the soup to the blender, add in the avocado flesh and the lime juice and blitz again. Pour into a bowl and cover the surface of the liquid with Clingfilm to keep it in perfect condition and chill completely.

Serve ice cold with a garnish of thinly sliced cucumber and a sprig of watercress.

## UP TO DATE

*Opposite*: Two recent TV adverts for Horlicks. 'How Does He Sleep At Night?' was a series of ads featuring mischevious acts. Their Horlicks-drinking perpetrators were able to sleep at ease though! The 'Made For Evenings' series simply showcased Horlicks as the perfect drink at the end of the day.

# Chicken, Bacon and Mushroom Pie

**This is a really lovely pie all year round, served hot in the winter or cold for summer picnics. Free-range chicken, malty Horlicks, salty bacon and earthy mushrooms make a brilliant combination.**

**SERVES 4**

1 large onion, peeled and diced
vegetable oil, for frying
450g free-range chicken breast, diced
1 teaspoon mixed herbs
100ml double cream
2 tablespoons **Horlicks Original powder**
150g closed cup mushrooms, wiped and quartered
2 rashers grilled back bacon, diced
375g ready-made shortcrust pastry
1 free-range medium egg, beaten
salt and black pepper

**You will need a buttered 20cm pie dish**

Sauté the onion in a little vegetable oil, then add the diced chicken. Cook, stirring a few times until the chicken is sealed all over, then add the herbs, cream and Horlicks and cook gently for 20 minutes. Next, add the mushrooms and bacon and cook for a further 10 minutes. Check the seasoning and add plenty of black pepper and salt if required. Remove from the heat and allow to cool.

Cut the pastry in half and roll out each on a floured board to make a base and a lid. Line the dish with the base pastry and then fill with the chicken mix mounding it in the centre, which makes it a better-looking pie when cooked. Moisten all round the top edges of the base pastry with water and then carefully lay the pastry lid over the top, pressing the edges together firmly to seal the pie.

Using the prongs of a fork, go right round the edge of the pie lip, making a series of indentations all the way round to decorate and help the seal. Cut out some leaf shapes from the pastry trimmings, brush them with water and fix them in the centre of the pie lid for decoration. Now brush the whole pie with beaten egg and pierce 4 tiny slits in the top to release the steam. Bake in the centre of the oven for 25 minutes or until golden brown.

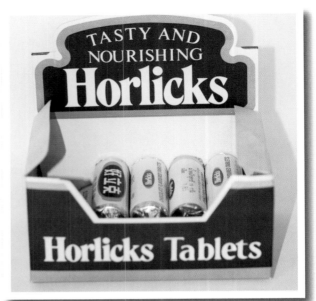

Horlicks

# Acknowledgements

This has been a real experience and a great privilege to write the recipes for the *Horlicks Cookbook*. I have cooked with Horlicks for years and the joy of using this iconic malty brand to infuse and build flavours has been incredibly good fun. I would like to thank my team of chefs at Hartley's Kitchen who have worked closely with me, first my darling wife, Lynda, whose enthusiasm has no bounds, then Joss Bechim-Horton who has worked diligently to perfect my savoury recipes, often in a manor that surprised even me – Joss you have been terrific! And Beth Rowe, our dessert specialist, who has turned ideas of sweet Horlicks recipes into truly great dishes.

Then there are our chums who come to supper not knowing what to expect and have been such wonderful supporters of guessing games about which dish has Horlicks in it. It has been a revelation and I can't tell you how much I have enjoyed writing this book. Finally I have to mention Bentley, my Horlicks-coloured Labrador, who has done his fair share of recipe tasting.

Then to my ever-faithful publishers at Absolute Press. Firstly, Jon Croft, who was such an encouragement and backed up my creativity with food in a stalwart manner. Then the graphics and overall elegance of this book is thanks to Matt Inwood – a truly creative art director – and to Andrea who has kept the pace going. Finally, my sincere thanks to Jane Leeds at Horlicks who believed in my ability to build Horlicks into culinary ingredients – thank you Jane: I hope you are as pleased as I am with this book.

Absolute Press would like to thank Jane Leeds, Sandi Boyden, Elias Kupfermann and all at Glaxo Smithkline who have helped with the production of this book. With thanks also to Robert Opie for providing archive material from his collection.